HOW WELL DO YOU KNOW THE HOLY BIBLE?

Bible Trivia

Volume II

RAYFORD J. ELLIOTT

This book is a work of non-fiction. All scriptures were taken from the KJV, NIV, ESV, NKJV of the Holy Bible but are not noted.

CLF Publishing, LLC
www.clfpublishing.org
909.315.3161

Copyright © 2021 by Rayford Jones Elliott. All right reserved. No portion of this book may be reproduced, stored in a retrieval system, or transmitted by any form of any means electronically, photocopied, recorded, or any other except for brief questions in printer reviews, without prior permission of the publisher.

ISBN #978-1-945102-67-7

Cover designed by Rayford J. Elliott

Printed in the United States of America.

Dedication

This book is dedicated to all the Sunday school students who come every week with an open mind and heart to learn more of the Word of God. They diligently study every week and prepare to grab all they can from the teachings and discussions to strengthen their relationship with God. As a matter of fact, this is how the idea of writing a book with trivia questions, brief commentary, and the supporting scriptures came about.

Every week, in addition to the study material we use, I text five trivia questions to the students. As a result, we have found it is a great tool to use to enhance their learning. I urge our Sunday school students at my church and all churches to continue to study to show yourselves approved. As II Timothy tells us in 2:15: *"Study to shew thyself approved unto God, a workman that needeth not to be ashamed, rightly dividing the word of truth."*

Preface

This book was written with the intent to help build one's relationship with God through learning more about Him through His Word. It is a book of trivia questions, with comments, and scriptures to support the answers. It came out of the trivia questions I give my Sunday school students. Each week, I text them five trivia questions to help enhance their studies of the Word of God.

Sunday school is an important ministry in the church today, which is a means of educating believers building a stronger relationship with God. Sunday school started in the 1780's and was primarily for kids. This is no longer the case; it is now for adults as well as kids. Most churches today have sessions for children, young adults, and adults.

The basic foundation of the church is witnessing. That is what built the early church. The knowledge of God and your testimony together are powerful weapons for winning souls to God.

I hope you will find this book useful in increasing your knowledge and understanding through these trivia questions, explanations, and supported scriptures. *"And that from a child thou hast known the holy scriptures, which are able to make thee wise unto salvation through faith which is in Christ Jesus"* (II Timothy 3:15).

Introduction

There is only one book in the world that you can study all your life and continue to learn. With other books, you read them to learn their principles, and that is about the extent of it; they are no longer needed, and you go on to the next one. However, the Bible is non-exhaustive with the lessons it teaches. As you study and read it, there is always something else that will be revealed to you by the Holy Spirit. It is the Book of Life; therefore, throughout your life, you will need it for your daily living. It provides you with principals and doctrines for living your life socially, politically, economically, psycho-logically, and above all spiritually. Thus, the question is, "Do you know the Bible?" There are many ways you can read it: vaingloriously, literally, and spiritually.

To read vaingloriously means it is read and studied to receive glory from others. Reading literally is to read and study to get the essence of it to use it as correctly as possible to adhere to what is being taught. Reading the Bible spiritually is the best way to read. When you read it spiritually, you read it with expectancy. You know it has answers for your daily living. The spiritual will supersede all other methods. It has all the answers through justification, sanctification, and salvation. We all need to be justified, sanctified and saved by our Lord and Savior Jesus Christ. The Bible tells us how that can be done.

Like many things in life, the more knowledge and understanding you have, the better you can cling to what the Bible is telling you. So, do you know the Bible?

Unlike any other book, the Bible is not just a book of knowledge; rather, it is also a book of relationship. Thus, we all can build and strengthen our relationship with God. Like any relationship, the more you associate and communicate with God's Word, the stronger the relationship. This relationship manifests itself with the Word of God, which is the Bible.

This book is designed to help you build your relationship with God. It is done by using trivia questions, which will capture your interest and curiosity by the use of various biblical facts and stories. Good questions have a tendency to attract and create a sense of wonder and curiosity. That is what this book will create in you, so that your relationship with God grows stronger, as you receive the amazing Word of God.

This book is limited in the number of questions that it contains. After all, there are literally thousands of questions that can be asked. As such, I speculate there will be a series of books in this format to come in the near future.

May the grace of God continue to be with you, and may His blessings continue to rain down on you.

God bless!!

Which two men in the Bible did God say they were not to cut their hair with a razor?

A Nazarite is the name for Israelites who made vows as prescribed in Numbers 6:2-21. They were to be separated from others and consecrated to God. There were several vows that were taken. One of them was not to shave their hair with a razor. Sampson and Samuel were the two that were mentioned.

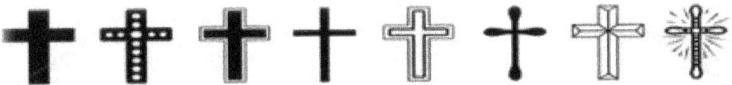

Sampson- *"For, lo, thou shalt conceive, and bear a son; and no razor shall come on his head: for the child shall be a Nazarite unto God from the womb: and he shall begin to deliver Israel out of the hand of the Philistines"* Judges 13:5.

Samuel- *"And she was in bitterness of soul, and prayed unto the LORD, and wept sore. And she vowed a vow, and said, O LORD of hosts, if thou wilt indeed look on the affliction of thine handmaid, and remember me, and not forget thine handmaid, but wilt give unto thine handmaid a man child, then I will give him unto the LORD all the days of his life, and there shall no razor come upon his head"* 1 Samuel 1:10-11.

Who had the skills, talent and understanding that was sent to help build the Temple?

It was Huram-abi. He was a man that was multi-talented in working with gold, silver, bronze, iron, stone and wood. Also, he was skillful in working with purple, blue and crimson yarn and fine linen. Thus, one can see he was an asset in the building of the temple because all these skills and talents were a necessary component in the construction of the temple.

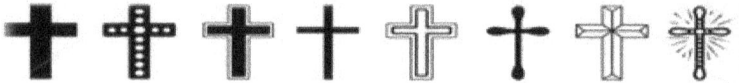

"Now I have sent a skilled man, who has understanding, Huram-abi, the son of a woman of the daughters of Dan, and his father was a man of Tyre. He is trained to work in gold, silver, bronze, iron, stone, and wood, and in purple, blue, and crimson fabrics and fine linen, and to do all sorts of engraving and execute any design that may be assigned him, with your craftsmen, the craftsmen of my lord, David your father" 2 Chronicles 2:13-15.

How many porters, stonecutters and supervisors did Solomon assign to build the temple?

The Temple was not a very big building. As a matter of fact, it was 150 feet long and 75 feet wide. With such a small size, it is amazing that it had so many people and so much material to build it. Solomon used 70,000 porters, 80,000 stonecutters and 3,600 supervisors in addition to the other skillful people used. But that was God's house, and it had to be made to perfection for Him to dwell in.

"*Now Solomon purposed to build a house for the Name of the LORD and a royal palace for himself. 2So he conscripted 70,000 porters, 80,000 stonecutters in the mountains, and 3,600 supervisors*" 2 Chronicles 2:1.

Who will become a world leader and attempt to get the world to worship Satan and believe Satan's lies?

In the End Times, there is a period called The Great Tribulation. It will last for seven years. The first three and a half years of this seven-year period will focus on one man who is called the Antichrist as the world leader. The Antichrist will promote the lies of Satan and try to convince everyone that there isn't or never was a Jesus Christ.

"Who is the liar but he who denies that Jesus is the Christ? This is the antichrist, he who denies the Father and the Son" 1 John 2:22.

"For many deceivers have gone out into the world, those who do not confess the coming of Jesus Christ in the flesh. Such a one is the deceiver and the antichrist" 2 John 1:7.

How many men in the Bible did God tell to write what He said down?

Throughout the Bible, you will find that God spoke to may men. However, He communicated with them in different ways. It may have been through a vision, a dream or by directly speaking to them. But there were a few that he spoke to and instructed them to write down what he had said. They were Jeremiah, John in Revelation, Moses, Ezekiel, Isaiah and Habakkuk.

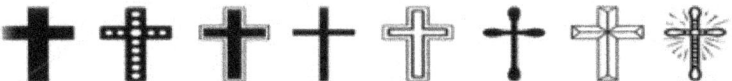

"Thus speaketh the LORD *God of Israel, saying, Write thee all the words that I have spoken unto thee in a book"* Jeremiah 30:2.

"Saying, I am Alpha and Omega, the first and the last: and, What thou seest, write in a book, and send it unto the seven churches which are in Asia" Revelation 1:11.

"Now go, write it before them in a table, and note it in a book that it may be for the time to come for ever and ever" Isaiah 30:8. Also: Ezekiel 9:2; Habakkuk 2:2; Moses-Exodus 34:27.

Which apostle was at the cross when Jesus died?

By the time of Jesus' crucifixion, it was no doubt that all of his apostles were known. And, of course, they feared for their life. But there were four disciples and one apostle that was there at the crucifixion. There were four women who followed and believed in Him: Mary, Jesus' mother; her sister; Mary, wife of Clopas; and Mary Magdalene. The apostle was John. When Jesus saw His mother and the disciple He loved (which is John) standing nearby, He addressed His mother.

"But standing by the cross of Jesus were his mother and his mother's sister, Mary the wife of Clopas, and Mary Magdalene" John 19:25.

*"*When Jesus saw his mother and the disciple whom he loved standing nearby, he said to his mother, 'Woman, behold, your son!'"* John 16:26.

Rayford J. Elliott

Who did the Lord select to help Moses to manage and bear the burden of all the Israelites on their way to the Promise Land?

Moses led the Israelites out of Egypt. During that time of leading the people, they became a big burden on him. People were making demands, murmuring, losing faith and rebelling against the leadership of Moses. God saw it necessary to give him help in dealing with the thousands of people he had to manage. He had Moses to choose seventy elders to be anointed to become his helpers.

"Then the LORD said to Moses, "Gather for me seventy men of the elders of Israel, whom you know to be the elders of the people and officers over them, and bring them to the tent of meeting, and let them take their stand there with you. [17] And I will come down and talk with you there. And I will take some of the Spirit that is on you and put it on them, and they shall bear the burden of the people with you, so that you may not bear it yourself alone" Numbers 11:16-17.

Who did Paul stay with when he returned to Jerusalem after three years in Asia?

After Paul was converted, he was led by the spirit to go to Asia Minor. He lived there for three years. During that time, he studied the Word of God and prepared himself for the ministry messages he was called to give. After he left Asia, he went to Jerusalem. There, he met with Peter and spent 15 days staying in Peter's house.

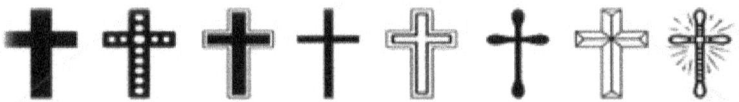

"Then after three years I went up to Jerusalem to see Peter, and abode with him fifteen days" Galatians 1:18.

Rayford J. Elliott

What did God use to symbolize the covenant between Him and Abraham?

When Abraham was ninety-nine years old, God made His first appearance to him. The covenant between God and Abraham was established in this encounter. And God gave him instructions on what Abraham needed to do to symbolize the covenant. He was to circumcise every male born including his male servants. That was the sign to remind him of the established covenant between them.

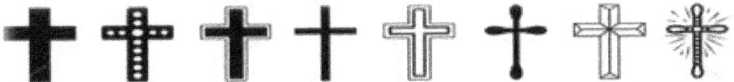

"*And ye shall circumcise the flesh of your foreskin; and it shall be a token of the covenant betwixt me and you. And he that is eight days old shall be circumcised among you, every man child in your generations, he that is born in the house, or bought with money of any stranger, which is not of thy seed. He that is born in thy house, and he that is bought with thy money, must needs be circumcised: and my covenant shall be in your flesh for an everlasting covenant*" Genesis 17:11-14.

Who wrapped Jesus' body in cloth after He was taken down from the cross?

After Jesus died on the cross, there was a man who had great respect for Him. That man was Joseph from Arimathea. With the love, respect and as a disciple of Jesus, Joseph went to Pilate and requested Jesus' body. Upon receiving the body of Jesus, he took it and wrapped it in clean linen. He then took his body to the tomb he had reserved and laid Jesus in it. When he was done, he rolled back the stone at the entrance of the tomb.

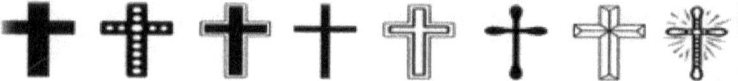

"When the even was come, there came a rich man of Arimathaea, named Joseph, who also himself was Jesus' disciple: He went to Pilate, and begged the body of Jesus. Then Pilate commanded the body to be delivered. And when Joseph had taken the body, he wrapped it in a clean linen cloth" Matthew 27:59.

Rayford J. Elliott

How many disciples did Jesus give the Great Commission to and where?

Jesus' Great Commission is to go into the world and teach to all nations the gospel and baptize each person in the name of the Father, the Son, and the Holy Ghost. He gave the commission to the eleven apostles. That took place on a mountain in Galilee where Jesus had appointed them as apostles.

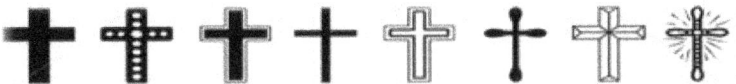

"Then the eleven disciples went away into Galilee, into a mountain where Jesus had appointed them. And when they saw him, they worshipped him: but some doubted. And Jesus came and spake unto them, saying, All power is given unto me in heaven and in earth. Go ye therefore, and teach all nations, baptizing them in the name of the Father, and of the Son, and of the Holy Ghost" Matthew 28:16-19.

What did Jesus declare before He gave the Great Commission to the disciples?

Jesus demonstrated, from the beginning of His ministry to His death on the wooden cross, the power God had bestowed up on Him. Wherever He went, His power was demonstrated, from turning water into wine, casting out demons, calming the sea, and more. However, some yet doubted Him. As He met with the eleven disciples, He declared "All Power" had been given to Him in heaven and on earth.

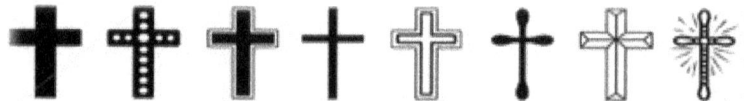

"Then the eleven disciples went away into Galilee, into a mountain where Jesus had appointed them. And when they saw him, they worshipped him: but some doubted. And Jesus came and spake unto them, saying, All power is given unto me in heaven and in earth" Matthew 28:16-18.

What was Paul's first miracle?

When Paul and Barnabus, along with John, started on their second mission, they stopped and preached on the island of Cyprus. There, they met a false prophet/magician Elymus who spoke against the true gospel of Jesus Christ. Paul rebuked his teaching. Paul being filled with the Holy Spirit caused Elymus to go blind. That happened immediately in the front of all the city councils and other leaders. When they saw that, they believed. That was the first miracle Paul performed.

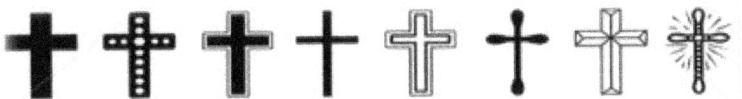

"And now, behold, the hand of the Lord is upon thee, and thou shalt be blind, not seeing the sun for a season. And immediately there fell on him a mist and a darkness; and he went about seeking some to lead him by the hand. Then the deputy, when he saw what was done, believed, being astonished at the doctrine of the Lord" Acts 13:11-12.

How was Isaiah's sin atoned?

When Isaiah was called by God, he was hesitant about answering that call because he had sin in his life and didn't think he was worthy of such a call. He said he was a man of unclean lips, which implies he used filthy language. So, God sent an angel (seraphim) to clean him. The angel held live coal in his hand from the altar and laid it upon his lips. Afterward, Isaiah's iniquity and sin were purged out of him.

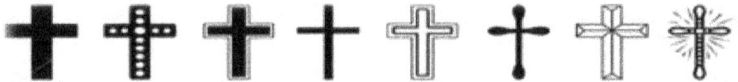

"Then said I, Woe is me! for I am undone; because I am a man of unclean lips, and I dwell in the midst of a people of unclean lips: for mine eyes have seen the King, the LORD of hosts. Then flew one of the seraphims unto me, having a live coal in his hand, which he had taken with the tongs from off the altar: And he laid it upon my mouth, and said, Lo, this hath touched thy lips; and thine iniquity is taken away, and thy sin purged" Isaiah 6:5-7.

Where was Jesus when the people against Him attempted to throw Him off a cliff?

Nazareth was Jesus' home town. And that city for a time was a headquarter for Jesus. The people knew Him and were familiar with Him, but most of them rejected His teaching. While He was teaching in the synagogue, the people became furious about what He was teaching: He was teaching that the Prophesy had been fulfilled, which was Him, and He gave examples from Old Testament scriptures how God was good to the Gentiles. They became so infuriated until they drove Him out of town near a cliff. There, they attempted to push Him off the cliff, but Jesus just walked through them and the people became petrified.

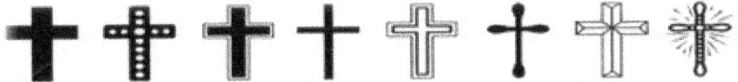

"All the people in the synagogue were furious when they heard this. they got up, drove him out of the town, and took him to the brow of the hill on which the town was built, in order to throw him off the cliff. But he walked right through the crowd and went on his way" Luke 4:28-30.

Who were the two gentiles Jesus used in the Old Testament as an example of how God blessed Jews as well as Gentiles?

Jesus taught in the Synagogue in Nazareth that Naaman, a Syrian who had leprosy, was healed by Elijah and the widow woman who was not a Jew had been stricken by a three-and-a-half-year famine was miraculously provided food throughout the remainder of the famine after she had supplied Elisha with one meal of bread. Jesus taught that the Jews cannot be exclusive for salvation but salvation is for all.

"I assure you that there were many widows in Israel in Elijah's time, when the sky was shut for three and a half years and there was a severe famine throughout the land. Yet Elijah was not sent to any of them, but to a widow in Zarephath in the region of Sidon. And there were many in Israel with leprosy in the time of Elisha the prophet, yet not one of them was cleansed—only Naaman the Syrian" Luke 4:24-27. Note - 1 Kings 17:7-16, 2 Kings 5:6-13.

Rayford J. Elliott

What name did God give to Jacob?

When Jacob prepared to meet his brother Esau to try to mend their relationship, he sent gifts ahead before they met. Since he was camped relatively close by Esau's camp, he sent his two wives and eleven sons ahead. He was left alone. That night, he wrestled with a man and would not let him go. When the man saw that Jacob was not going to let him go, he took out Jacob's hip joint, but Jacob still would not release him. He said to the man that he would not release him until he blessed him. The man then changed Jacob's name to Israel. That man was God.

"So Jacob was left all alone, and there a man wrestled with him until day break. When the man saw that He could not overpower Jacob, He struck the socket of Jacob's hip and dislocated it as they wrestled. Then the man said, "Let Me go, for it is daybreak." But Jacob replied, "I will not let You go unless You bless me." "What is your name?" the man asked. "Jacob," he replied. Then the man said, "Your name will no longer be Jacob, but Israel, because you have struggled with God and with men, and you have prevailed" Genesis 32:28.

What happened when the two men who walked with Jesus on the Emmaus road finally realized who He is?

The day Jesus rose from the tomb, He joined two men walking on the road to Emmaus. As the three walked, they told Jesus about the crucifixion, assuming Jesus was not aware what had taken place. Jesus then began to talk to them on what the Scripture says about the Prophesy and His death. When they approached the village, they asked Jesus to stay with them. When they broke bread with Him that evening, they finally realized who He is. Jesus then vanished from their sight.

"And they drew nigh unto the village, whither they went: and he made as though he would have gone further. But they constrained him, saying, Abide with us: for it is toward evening, and the day is far spent. And he went in to tarry with them. And it came to pass, as he sat at meat with them, he took bread, and blessed it, and brake, and gave to them. And their eyes were opened, and they knew him; and he vanished out of their sight" Luke 24:28-31.

Rayford J. Elliott

Which sons were born by Rachel, the wife whom Jacob love?

Jacob had twelve sons and one daughter. They came by way of four wives. By his first wife, Leah, he had Reuben, the oldest, then Simeon, Levi, Judah, Issachar, Zebulon and a daughter Dinah. By Bilhah, Rachel's servant, he had Dan and Naphtali. By Zilpah, Leah's servant, he had Gad and Asher. And by the wife he loved, Rachel, he had Joseph and Benjamin, Benjamin being the youngest one.

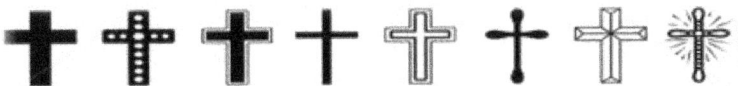

"And Leah conceived, and bare a son, and she called his name Reuben". Gen 29:32. *"and she called his name Simeon."* Gen 29:33. *"his name called Levi."* Gen 29:34. *"he called his name Judah."* Gen. 29:35. *"Bilhah conceived, and bare Jacob a son"..."called she his name Dan."* Geb:30:6 *"called his name Naphtali."* Gen 30:8. *"Zilpah Leah's maid bare Jacob a son."* Gen. 30:10. *"she called his name Gad".* Gen. 30:11. *"she called his name Asher."* Gen 30:13. *"unto Leah, and she conceived,"* .. *"his name Issachar."* Gen 30:18. *"called his name Zebulun."* Gen. 30:20. *"a daughter, and called her name/Dinah."* Gen 30:21... *"Rachel,..she conceived, and bare a son*; Gen. 30:23. *"name Joseph;"* Gen. 30:24. *"called him Benjamin"* Gen. 35:18.

25

What was the first recorded war in the Bible?

The war of the "nine kings." Four kings were from Mesopotamia, and five were below the Dead Sea, which included Sodom (where Lot lived) and Gomorrah and three other kings. The four kings from the north defeated Sodom and Gomorrah and the other three kings. Lot and his family were taken captive. Also, all of the gold, silver, servants and women were taken. When Abraham heard about the defeat and the capture of his nephew Lot, he immediately organized 318 of his servants and pursued the four nations and defeated them, rescued Lot and returned all that was taken from Sodom and Gomorrah. Abraham gave it all back to these nations.

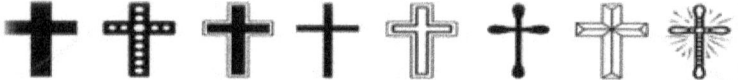

"And it came to pass in the days of Amraphel king of Shinar, Arioch king of Ellasar, Chedorlaomer king of Elam, and Tidal king of nations; That these made war with Bera king of Sodom, and with Birsha king of Gomorrah, Shinab king of Admah, and Shemeber king of Zeboiim, and the king of Bela, which is Zoar" Genesis 14:1-2.

Rayford J. Elliott

Why was there hatred between the Jews and Samaritans?

The Samaritans were a product of the Jews intermarriage with the Gentiles, namely the Assyrians, after Assyria captured the northern kingdom of Israel in 721 BC. After the capture, some of the people from the nation of Israel stayed behind and married the Assyrians. Their intermarriage produced offspring, which the Bible designates as the Samaritans. However, there was a city called Samaria, and this is where it all took place under the Assyrian's rule. Since this act was a direct violation of the Jewish law, Jews did not want to associate with them because they were considered not pure in their eyes.

"*In the ninth year of Hoshea, the king of Assyria captured Samaria and deported the Israelites to Assyria. He settled them in Halah, in Gozan on the Habor River and in the towns of the Medes. All this took place because the Israelites had sinned against the LORD their God, who had brought them up out of Egypt from under the power of Pharaoh king of Egypt. They worshiped other gods and followed the practices of the nations the LORD had driven out before them, as well as the practices that the kings of Israel had introduced*" 2 Kings 17:6-8, 24.

What was Joseph interpretation of Pharaoh's dream?

Joseph was given the gift of dream interpretation by God. When he was in prison, he helped many people with his gift. After he was set free, he had the opportunity to interpret a dream for Pharaoh, the king of Egypt. He gave a description of Pharaoh's dream and broke it down, so he could understand it. In the final interpretation, he told Pharaoh there will be a severe famine in the land.

"Behold, there come seven years of great plenty throughout all the land of Egypt: And there shall arise after them seven years of famine; and all the plenty shall be forgotten in the land of Egypt; and the famine shall consume the land; And the plenty shall not be known in the land by reason of that famine following; for it shall be very grievous." Genesis 41:29-31.

Rayford J. Elliott

What did the soldiers at Jesus' crucifixion do with Jesus' robe?

When Jesus was being prepared to be crucified, Pilate wrote on the cross "Jesus of Nazareth, the king of the Jews." The high priest objected to this notice writing, but Pilate kept it. And the soldiers took Jesus' robe and they wanted to cut it into four parts but decided not to. Instead, they cast lots to see who would get it. That was a fulfillment of the Scripture (Psalm 22:18).

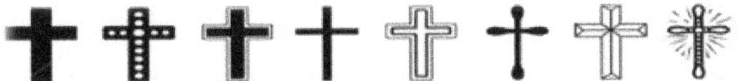

"And Pilate wrote a title, and put it on the cross. And the writing was Jesus of Nazareth the king of the Jews. This title then read many of the Jews: for the place where Jesus was crucified was nigh to the city: and it was written in Hebrew, and Greek, and Latin. Then said the chief priests of the Jews to Pilate, Write not, The King of the Jews; but that he said, I am King of the Jews. Pilate answered, What I have written I have written. Then the soldiers, when they had crucified Jesus, took his garments, and made four parts, to every soldier a part; and also his coat: now the coat was without seam, woven from the top throughout. They said therefore among themselves, Let us not rend it, but cast lots for it, whose it shall be: that the scripture might be fulfilled," John 19:19-24.

Which book has the least number of chapters in the Old Testament?

The book of Obadiah is written concerning the divine judgment of Edom and the restoration of Israel. It was written during the Assyrians' reign. Obadiah was a prophet. The book consists of a single chapter, which no other book written in the Old Testament has. It is divided into twenty-one verses, which makes it the shortest.

"The vision of Obadiah. Thus saith the Lord Go concerning Edom; We have heard a rumour from the LORD, and an ambassador is sent among the heathen, Arise ye, and let us rise up against her in battle. Behold, I have made thee small among the heathen: thou art greatly despised" Obadiah 1:1-2.

"And the captivity of this host of the children of Israel shall possess that of the Canaanites, even unto Zarephath; and the captivity of Jerusalem, which is in Sepharad, shall possess the cities of the south. And saviours shall come up on mount Zion to judge the mount of Esau; and the kingdom shall be the LORD's:" Obadiah 1:20-21.

Who was the first person to come upon the injured man in the parable of the Good Samaritan?

This is an interesting, popular parable. It shows that sometime people that are in certain positions don't always have the quality of brotherly love. There were three men who passed by a man who was injured on his way from Jerusalem to Jericho. He who had been robbed and beaten. Only one of the three stopped to help him. The first one was a priest, the second one was a Levite, and the third one was a Samaritan, who was from a nation of people that the Jews despised during that time; and he was the only one who stopped to help the injured man.

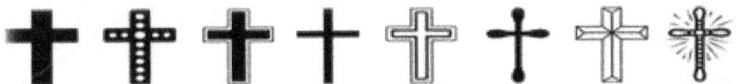

"A man was going down from Jerusalem to Jericho, and he fell among robbers, who stripped him and beat him and departed, leaving him half dead. Now by chance a priest was going down that road, and when he saw him he passed by on the other side. So likewise a Levite, when he came to the place and saw him, passed by on the other side. But a Samaritan, as he journeyed, came to where he was, and when he saw him, he had compassion. He went to him and bound up his wounds, pouring on oil and wine. Then he set him on his own animal and brought him to an inn and took care of him" Luke 10:30-34.

Which tribe was Paul from?

Paul was one of the most popular contributing apostles in the New Testament. As an apostle, he was selected by our Lord and Savior Jesus Christ. He wrote approximately one third of the New Testament. As an apostle, he met all the three criteria the early church defined for an apostle. Peter, who was the leader of the church at that time, with the council formulated these criteria (Acts 1:21-26). Paul, before he became a Christian, was part of the Jewish Sec, the Pharisees. All of the Jewish Pharisees were descendants of the twelve tribes. In Paul's case, he was a descendant from the Benjamin tribes, who was the youngest son of Jacob.

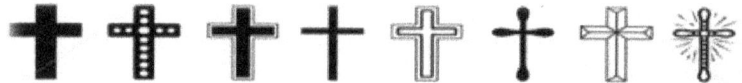

"I say then, Has God cast away his people? God forbid. For I also am an Israelite, of the seed of Abraham, of the tribe of Benjamin" **Romans 11:1.**

Rayford J. Elliott

Who did God save before the cities of Sodom and Gomorrah were destroyed?

The cities of Sodom and Gomorrah are prime examples of how destructive sin can be. These cities were so deep in sin until it brought on the wrath of God to destroy them. Lot, who dwelled in Sodom, was accosted by two angels in his home to inform him of the destruction to come upon these cities. They informed him what was about to occur and that he and his family could be spared if they would leave before the destruction. Lot gathered himself, his wife and two daughters and left the city. There were four people saved from the destruction.

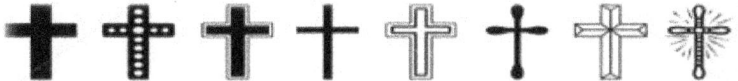

"*As morning dawned, the angels urged Lot, saying, "Up! Take your wife and your two daughters who are here, lest you be swept away in the punishment of the city." But he lingered. So the men seized him and his wife and his two daughters by the hand, the LORD being merciful to him, and they brought him out and set him outside the city*" Genesis 19:15-16.

What did the Israelites write on the uncut stone or the altar they built after they first entered the Promise Land across the Jordan?

Moses and the elders did not live to see the Promise Land. However, they did instruct the people to build an altar when they initially possessed the land. The law God had given to them was of the utmost importance, and the people were to always obey and live by the law. Their instruction was to use uncut stones to build the altar. They were to offer bunt offerings and to write on the stones all the words of the law that was given to them by Moses.

"*And there shalt thou build an altar unto the LORD thy God, an altar of stones: thou shalt not lift up any iron tool upon them. Thou shalt build the altar of the LORD thy God of whole stones: and thou shalt offer burnt offerings thereon unto the LORD thy God: And thou shalt offer peace offerings, and shalt eat there, and rejoice before. the LORD thy God. And thou shalt write upon the stones all the words of this law very plainly*" Deuteronomy 27:6-8.

Rayford J. Elliott

How did Judas signal Jesus' identity to the Roman officials?

Jesus was arrested because of the betrayal of one of his disciples. The one who betrayed him had been with him since the beginning of His ministry. It was Judas Iscariot, who betrayed Jesus for a few pieces of silver. On that evening, when the arrest took place, Judas was to signal the soldiers by a kiss. His kissing Jesus was the way he had planned to identify Jesus to the Romans. However, Jesus knew it was a kiss of betrayal.

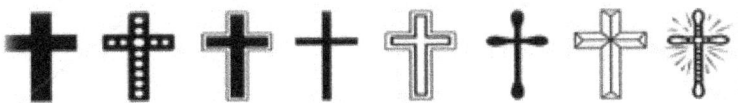

"And being in an agony he prayed more earnestly: and his sweat was as it were great drops of blood falling down to the ground And when he rose up from prayer, and was come to his disciples, he found them sleeping for sorrow, And said unto them, Why sleep ye? rise and pray, lest ye enter into temptation. And while he yet spake, behold a multitude, and he that was called Judas, one of the twelve, went before them, and drew near unto Jesus to kiss him. But Jesus said unto him, Judas, betrayest thou the Son of man with a kiss" Luke 22:44-48.

How Well Do You Know the Holy Bible?

How many times did the Lord call Samuel?

Samuel was a young boy when the Lord called him. He was under the apprenticeship of Eli, and one night while he was asleep, the voice of God called his name. He awakened and went to Eli several times. Eli told him each time he did not call him. The Lord called him four times before he realized that it was the Lord who called him, not Eli.

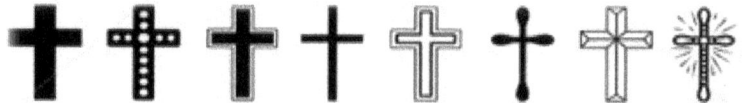

"That the LORD called Samuel. And he answered, "Here I am!" So he ran to Eli and said, "Here I am, for you called me." And he said, "I did not call; lie down again." And he went and lay down. Then the LORD called yet again, "Samuel!" So Samuel arose and went to Eli, and said, "Here I am, for you called me." He answered, "I did not call, my son; lie down again." (Now Samuel did not yet know the LORD, nor was the word of the LORD yet revealed to him.) And the LORD called Samuel again the third time. So he arose and went to Eli, and said, "Here I am, for you did call me." Then Eli perceived that the LORD had called the boy. Therefore Eli said to Samuel, "Go, lie down; and it shall be, if He calls you, that you must say, 'Speak, LORD, for Your servant hears.' "So Samuel went and lay down in his place. Now the LORD came and stood and called as at other times, "Samuel! Samuel!" And Samuel answered, "Speak, for Your servant hears" 1 Samuel 3:4-10.

Rayford J. Elliott

In which city was Paul and Silas imprisoned during their second missionary journey?

When Paul and Silas were in Philippi, they met a demon-possessed girl who was being used by her master for financial gain. She verbally attacked Paul about who he was and who he represented (Jesus). Paul prayed and cast the demon out of her. Her master heard about what Paul did and made accusations against Paul and Silas to the magistrate. They were arrested, whipped and jailed in the city of Philippi.

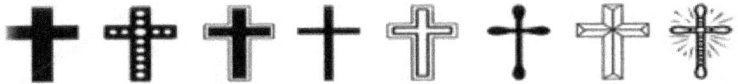

"And this did she many days. But Paul, being grieved, turned and said to the spirit, I command thee in the name of Jesus Christ to come out of her. And he came out the same hour. And when her masters saw that the hope of their gains was gone, they caught Paul and Silas, and drew them into the marketplace unto the rulers" Acts 16:18-19.

"And the multitude rose up together against them: and the magistrates rent off their clothes, and commanded to beat them. And when they had laid many stripes upon them, they cast them into prison, charging the jailor to keep them safely: Who, having received such a charge, thrust them into the inner prison, and made their feet fast in the stocks" Acts 16:22-24.

What was the name of Adam's third son?

Practically everyone on earth knows the story of Adam and his first two sons, Cain and Abel. Cain was a worker of the field, and Able was a worker of stock. They both were to present their labor products to the Lord. When Abel presented his product, the Lord was well pleased. Cain presented his, but it was not so pleasing to God. Cain became jealous of Abel's accomplishment and murdered him. Cain was banded and became a fugitive and a vagabond. Shortly after his departure, Adam and Eve bore another son and his name was Seth.

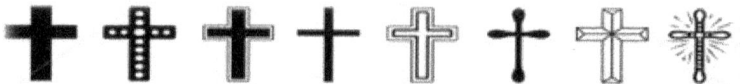

"And Adam knew his wife again; and she bare a son, and called his name Seth: For God, said she, hath appointed me another seed instead of Abel, whom Cain slew. And to Seth, to him also there was born a son; and he called his name Enos: then began men to call upon the name of the LORD" Genesis 4:25-26.

Rayford J. Elliott

What island was John on when he was given the vision of Revelation?

John was exiled by the Roman authorities because of his preaching of the Gospel of Jesus Christ. When he was exiled, he was the last remaining member of the twelve disciples. He was born in 6 AD. He was a close follower of Jesus Christ who also called him the disciple whom Jesus loved. He was captured in a Roman persecution campaign against the Christians. He ultimately, via his captivity, was sent to the island Patmos, which was an island where most criminals were sent. While he was there, he had a vision that was inspired by God to write the Book of Revelation.

"I John, who also am your brother, and companion in tribulation, and in the kingdom and patience of Jesus Christ, was in the isle that is called Patmos, for the word of God, and for the testimony of Jesus Christ. I was in the Spirit on the Lord's day, and heard behind me a great voice, as of a trumpet" Revelation 1:9-10.

Who is the only Gentile in the Bible to be identified as the Lord's anointed?

After the captivity and the destruction of the temple in Jerusalem, God planned the rebuilding of the temple. The people were still under the rule of the Persians. They had been in captivity for seventy years. The Persian king was Cyrus and reigned from 580 BC–529 BC. Since the people were still under their rule, they had to get permission from this oppressive nation to build the temple that had been destroyed. God selected King Cyrus to initiate the rebuilding of the temple. He became the shepherd for the Lord to accomplish this by anointing him as so.

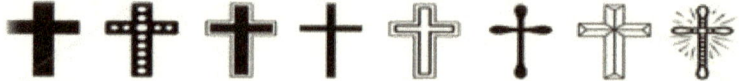

"Who says of Cyrus, He is my shepherd and will accomplish all that I please; he will say of Jerusalem, "Let it be rebuilt," and of the temple, "Let its foundations be laid" Isaiah 44:28.

"This is what the LORD says to his anointed, to Cyrus, whose right hand I take hold of to subdue nations before him and to strip kings of their armor, to open doors before him so that gates will not be shut" Isaiah 45:1.

Rayford J. Elliott

How many rivers were formed from the river that flowed out of Eden?

After God created man, He saw it was necessary to create a place for him to live and supply him food and other necessities for his life. He created a garden and named it Eden, which was capable of supplying man with all of his needs to live and for man to worship Him. And at the same time, there was a need to supply water. He created a river that flowed through eastward in Eden. From this river there were four rivers created from flowing out of Eden. The name of the four rivers are Pison, Giheon, Hiddekel and Euphrates.

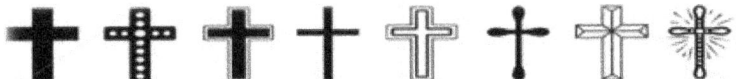

"And the LORD *God planted a garden eastward in Eden; and there he put the man whom he had formed. And out of the ground made the* LORD *God to grow every tree that is pleasant to the sight, and good for food; the tree of life also in the midst of the garden, and the tree of knowledge of good and evil. And a river went out of Eden to water the garden; and from thence it was parted, and became into four heads. The name of the first is Psion: that is it which compasseth the whole land of Havilah, where there is gold; And the gold of that land is good: there is bdellium and the onyx stone. And the name of the second river is Gihon: the same is it that compasseth the whole land of Ethiopia. And the name of the third river is Hiddekel: that is it which goeth toward the east of Assyria. And the fourth river is Euphrates"* Genesis 2:8-14.

Which prophet gave a warning to the people about oppressing the widows and the fatherless in the Bible?

The Lord spoke to many prophets. He gave messages to them to relay to the people for Him. Sometimes, the message is about a brighter future, the wrath of God coming upon them or God's mercy and grace being available. The people of Israel had been sinning all kinds of ways; the leadership was unfaithful, false worship was exercised, and there was oppression of their own people. One of the messages of God brought to the people by Malachi (a prophet) was a warning to the people for oppressing and abusing the widows and the fatherless.

"Then the gifts of Judah and Jerusalem will be pleasing to the Lord, as they were in the past. Then I will come to judge you. I will be quick to speak against those who use witchcraft, and those who do sex sins, and those who make false promises. I will speak against those who do not pay a man what he has earned, and who make it hard for the woman whose husband has died and for children who have no parents. And I will speak against those who turn away the stranger and do not fear Me," says the Lord of All. 'For I, the Lord, do not change. So you, O children of Jacob, are not destroyed" Malachi 3:4-6.

How many times was Peter told to forgive his brother who sinned against him?

While Jesus was teaching on forgiveness, He used the example of the unforgiving servant: A servant owed his master and begged him for relief because he did not have the money to pay him back. The master did not punish him for not being able to pay back at that time, but he had mercy on him and gave him more time. The servant had a brother who owed him, and he demanded payment, but his brother did not have the funds to repay him. He therefore had him put in jail. This servant did not have a forgiving heart even though his master showed him mercy. Peter asked Jesus the question on how often he should forgive. Jesus told him at least seven times and at the most seventy time seven, which translates into one should always show compassion and forgiveness.

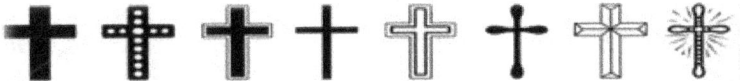

"Then came Peter to him, and said, Lord, how oft shall my brother sin against me, and I forgive him? till seven times? Jesus saith unto him, I say not unto thee, until seven times: but, Until seventy times seven" Matthew 18:22.

How long was Paul blind?

Paul (Saul) went to the high priest to ask for letters from the synagogues in Damascus to imprison anyone he found there belonging to the Way (the gospel). As he approached the city, suddenly a light from heaven flashed on him, and he fell to the ground, while hearing a voice saying, "Saul, Saul, why do you persecute Me?" The men traveling with him were speechless but heard the voice. Paul got up from the ground, but when he opened his eyes, he could not see. The men who heard the voice led him to Damascus. For three days, he was without sight, and he did not eat or drink anything.

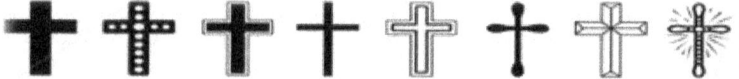

"And he trembling and astonished said, Lord, what wilt thou have me to do? And the Lord said unto him, Arise, and go into the city, and it shall be told thee what thou must do. And the men which journeyed with him stood speechless, hearing a voice, but seeing no man. And Saul arose from the earth; and when his eyes were opened, he saw no man: but they led him by the hand, and brought him into Damascus. And he was three days without sight, and neither did eat nor drink" Acts 9:6-9.

What was the name of the city founded by Cain?

Adam initially had two sons: Cain and Abel. Cain ended up killing his brother Abel. And his death is a result of Cain's jealously toward him simply because Abel's offering to the Lord was pleasing to God. Cain did not like the response that was given to his brother, and he set out to kill him. He murdered his brother out of jealously; there was no death penalty for such a crime at that time. Therefore, he was exiled from the family. When he was banded, he left to the east of Eden. He ended up finding a wife and had a son whom he named him Enoch. He built a city and named it Enoch.

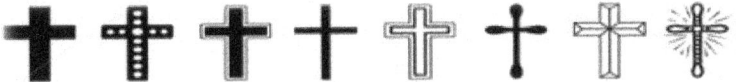

"But Cain said to the LORD, "My punishment is greater than I can bear. Behold, this day You have driven me from the face of the earth, and from Your face I will be hidden; I will be a fugitive and a wanderer on the earth, and whoever finds me will kill me." "Not so!" replied the LORD. "If anyone slays Cain, then Cain will be avenged sevenfold." And the LORD placed a mark on Cain, so that no one who found him would kill him. So Cain went out from the presence of the LORD and settled in the land of Nod, east of Eden. And Cain had relations with his wife, and she conceived and gave birth to Enoch. Then Cain built a city and named it after his son Enoch" Genesis 4:13-17.

How much hotter was the fiery furnace heated before Shadrach, Meshach, and Abednego were cast into the fire by King Nebuchadnezzar?

King Nebuchadnezzar made a golden statue sixty cubits high and six cubits wide, and he set it on the land of Dura, which is a part of Babylon. The king had a dedication and made a decree at a gathering. His decree stated that when all hear the sound of the horn and other instrument, everyone must fall down and worship this golden statue. All who did not do so would be thrown into the furnace. Shadrach, Meshach and Abednego were captive Jewish men who were caught up in the captivity by the Babylonians. They were strong believers and would only bow to the only true God. Their refusal to bow caused them to be cast into the fiery furnace. The king ordered it to be heated up seven times more than normal before they cast them into the fire.

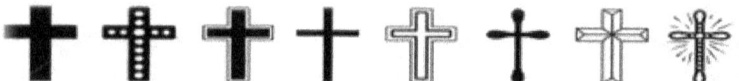

"At this, Nebuchadnezzar was filled with rage, and the expression on his face changed toward Shadrach, Meshach, and Abednego. He gave orders to heat the furnace seven times hotter than usual, and he commanded mighty warriors in his army to tie up Shadrach, Meshach, and Abednego and throw them into the burning fiery furnace" Daniel 3:19-20 (BSB).

Rayford J. Elliott

How was Korah and his followers punished for their rebellion against Moses and God?

When the Israelites first got to the Promise Land, Moses sent out twelve men to spy in the land for forty days. When they returned, only two had encouraging reports. The people went with the negative reports. For this reason, it caused them not to enter in the Promise Land at that time. They spent about forty years in the wilderness. During that time, Korah, a Levite, rebelled against Moses and God. Moses called an assembly and had Korah and his 250 followers separated from the masses of people. God allowed the earth to open up on the grounds that Korah and his followers stood. They all were instantly killed.

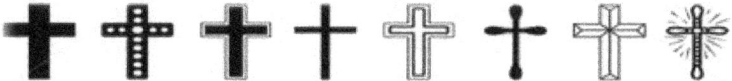

"As soon as he had finished saying all this, the ground under them split, and the earth opened up to swallow them, their families, the followers of Korah, and all their property. They went down alive to their graves with everything that belonged to them. The ground covered them, and so they disappeared from the assembly. All the Israelites around them ran away when they heard their screams. They thought the ground would swallow them, too" Numbers 16:31-34.

How many times did the Israelites send spies to spy in the Promise Land?

Before the Israelites left Egypt, God promised them a land to settle; it became known as the Promise Land. As they left, they ran into many obstacles. But by the grace and love of God, He protected and made sure all of their needs were met along the way. After a period of about a year and a half, they finally came to the land that was promised. They sent spies to gather information before they entered. They received some negative reports. Thus, they became afraid and lost their trust in God; as a result, they ended up in the wilderness for 38 years. When they returned, Joshua led them back to the river across the Promise Land and again sent two men to spy on the land. There were two instances.

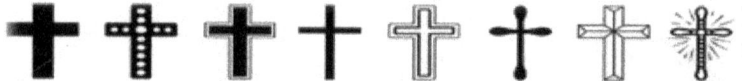

"And the LORD spake unto Moses, saying, Send thou men, that they may search the land of Canaan, which I give unto the children of Israel: of every tribe of their fathers shall ye send a man, everyone a ruler among them. And Moses by the commandment of Lord sent them from the wilderness of Paran: all those men were heads of the children of Israel" Numbers 13:1-3; Joshua 2:1.

"And Joshua the son of Nun sent out of Shittim two men to spy secretly, saying, Go view the land, even Jericho. And they went, and came into an harlot's house, named Rahab, and lodged there" Joshua 2:1.

Who were the only two survivors of the original 600,000 adult men who had left Egypt and entered the Promise Land?

The number of Israelites who left Egypt was approximately 600,000 men, excluding the women and children. They had traveled for two years before they arrived at the outskirts of the Promise Land. Because of fear and rebellion, they were not allowed to enter. As a matter of fact, God told them that all who were 20 years or older would die before they could enter the land. Therefore, God allowed them to wonder in the wilderness of sin for 38 years. They all died except Joshua and Caleb. They were the only ones who had left Egypt to see the Promise Land. However, there were thousands of the new generation.

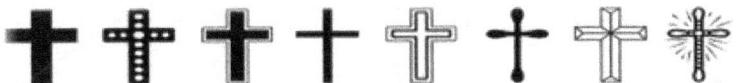

"In Numbers 14, verses 29-30, we read: "The carcasses of you who have complained against Me shall fall in this wilderness, all of you who were numbered, according to your entire number, from twenty years old and above. Except for Caleb the son of Jephunneh and Joshua the son of Nun, you shall by no means enter the land which I swore I would make you dwell" Numbers 14:29.

Who were the people that occupied the Promise Land before it was conquered?

God made His promise to the Israelites in Genesis 12 to Abraham. He said that the land of Canaan, the Promise Land would be Abraham's and all of his descendants. What's unique about the land is that it was a very fertile land with good soil to grow crops and raise herds. After Abraham possessed the land, he adobe there for a while and had to leave. Through Moses, the land was to be recaptured. In the Promised Land, there were many nations of people who were then occupying the land. They were the Canaanites, Hittites, Hivites, Perizzites, Girgashites, Amorites, and Jabusites.

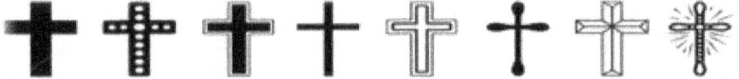

"And Joshua said, Hereby ye shall know that the living God is among you, and that he will without fail drive out from before you the Canaanites, and the Hittites, and the Hivites, and the Perizzites, and the Girgashites, and the Amorites, and the Jebusites" Joshua 3:10.

After the three temptations by Satan to Jesus, Jesus went to the temple, from whose scroll did he read to the Jews?

The temple was then, as well as now, a unique designated place for worship. However, worshiping God can be done anywhere, even in the midst of your enemies. The temple is a place of fellowshipping together by the saints. There are always customs and ceremonies that take place there. One of the customs was the reading of the scroll. As they gathered together, the Priest would read the scroll. On that special time, the high priest Jesus read the scroll. The scroll was read from the book of Isaiah. Isaiah's other name is Esaias.

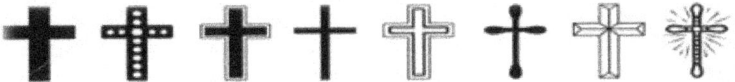

"And he came to Nazareth, where he had been brought up: and, as his custom was, he went into the synagogue on the sabbath day, and stood up for to read. And there was delivered unto him the book of the prophet Esaias. And when he had opened the book, he found the place where it was written, The Spirit of the Lord is upon me, because he hath anointed me to preach the gospel to the poor; he hath sent me to heal the brokenhearted, to preach deliverance to the captives, and recovering of sight to the blind, to set at liberty them that are bruised, To preach the acceptable year of the Lord" Luke 4:16-19.

How many men did the king allow the Ethiopian (Ebed-Malech) to take with him to pull Jeremiah out of the cistern?

King Zedekiah, the puppet king of Israel who was put in office by the Babylon king Nebuchadnezzar, imprisoned Jeremiah and had him thrown into a cistern. He was imprisoned because he gave a message from God that said the people should stop rebelling against Babylon and surrender, so they would live. The king was infuriated, so he arrested Jerimiah and threw him into a cistern because of what he had said. When he placed the order to take him out of the cistern, thirty men were assigned to rescue him.

"My lord the king, these men have acted wickedly in all they have done to Jeremiah the prophet. They have thrown him into a cistern, where he will starve to death when there is no longer any bread in the city." Then the king commanded Ebed-Melek the Cushite, "Take thirty men from here with you and lift Jeremiah the prophet out of the cistern before he dies." So Ebed-Melek took the men with him and went to a room under the treasury in the palace. He took some old rags and worn-out clothes from there and let them down with ropes to Jeremiah in the cistern. Ebed-Melek the Cushite said to Jeremiah, "Put these old rags and worn-out clothes under your arms to pad the ropes." Jeremiah did so, and they pulled him up with the ropes and lifted him out of the cistern. And Jeremiah remained in the courtyard of the guard" Jeremiah 38:9-12.

Rayford J. Elliott

How Well Do You Know the Holy Bible?

What similar occurrence do Jezebel, Ahab's wife, and Ahab had after their deaths?

Ahab was the king of Israel, the northern nation. His wife was Jezebel. They both were evil persons who worshipped pagan gods and were abusive to the people. Jehoshaphat was king of the southern nation. Both kings joined together to recaptured a nearby city that was seized by the Syrians. They went into battle, and Ahab was wounded. He died in his chariot on the way back home to Samaria. Dogs licked his blood that dripped from chariot he was carried in. When Jezebel was killed from being thrown out the windows by her own eunuchs, dogs licked her blood on the ground where she lay. Dogs licking their blood after their death is what was in common for Ahab and Jezebel after their deaths.

"And the LORD also speaks concerning Jezebel: 'The dogs will devour Jezebel by the wall of Jezreel.' He who belongs to Ahab and dies in the city will be eaten by dogs," 1 Kings 21:23,14. *"And the battle increased that day: and the king was stayed up in his chariot against the Syrians, and died at even: and the blood ran out of the wound into the midst of the chariot."* 1 Kings 22:35. *"So the king died, and was brought to Samaria; and they buried the king in Samaria.³⁸ And one washed the chariot in the pool of Samaria; and the dogs licked up his blood"* 1 Kings 22:37.

Rayford J. Elliott

When did an angel appear to Jesus and what did he do for Jesus?

When Jesus went to Mount Olive to the Garden of Gethsemane to pray, He took His disciples with Him. He was concerned about them and asked them to pray that they would not enter into temptation. At that moment, He asked God to remove the cup from Him. That was a low moment for Jesus. And suddenly, an Angel appeared to Him. The appearance of the angel strengthened Jesus.

"And when he was at the place, he said unto them, Pray that ye enter not into temptation. And he was withdrawn from them about a stone's cast, and kneeled down, and prayed, Saying, Father, if thou be willing, remove this cup from me: nevertheless not my will, but thine, be done. And there appeared an angel unto him from heaven, strengthening him" Luke 22:40-43.

While Jesus was ascending into heaven, the disciples watched. Who stood by them as they watched?

On the 40th day after Jesus' resurrection, He gathered with His disciples, and they asked Him when will the kingdom of Israel be restored? He told them it is not for them to know when. Then, Jesus ascended toward heaven. As the disciples watched Him ascend, there were two men (angels) beside them each wearing a white robe. They assured them that He will return.

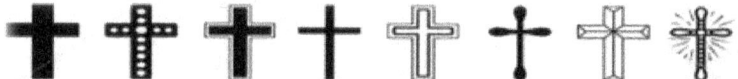

"But ye shall receive power, after that the Holy Ghost is come upon you: and ye shall be witnesses unto me both in Jerusalem, and in all Judaea, and in Samaria, and unto the uttermost part of the earth. And when he had spoken these things, while they beheld, he was taken up; and a cloud received him out of their sight. And while they looked stedfastly toward heaven as he went up, behold, two men stood by them in white apparel" Acts 1:8-10.

Rayford J. Elliott

Who caused the Israelite defeat in the battle at Ai?

After Jericho was taken, Joshua destroyed everything and put the gold, silver, articles and iron into the storehouse for the Lord. The next city they were to take was Ai. Joshua led the armed men to take the city, but they were unsuccessful. The reason was that someone had stolen from the house of the Lord. The guilty person was Achan; he had sinned against the Lord, and it affected the whole people.

"Up, sanctify the people, and say, Sanctify yourselves against to morrow: for thus saith the LORD *God of Israel, There is an accursed thing in the midst of thee, O Israel: thou canst not stand before thine enemies, until ye take away the accursed thing from among you"* Joshua 7:13.

"And Achan answered Joshua, and said, Indeed I have sinned against the LORD *God of Israel, and thus and thus have I done: When I saw among the spoils a goodly Babylonish garment, and two hundred shekels of silver, and a wedge of gold of fifty shekels weight, then I coveted them, and took them; and, behold, they are hid in the earth in the midst of my tent, and the silver under it"* Joshua 7:19-21.

What happened to the Philistine pagan god when they placed the Ark of the Covenant next to it?

The Israelites went to battle with the Philistines on two occasions. On each occasion, the Israelites were defeated. In the last battle, the Philistines took the Ark of the Covenant. With the Ark in their possession, they placed it beside their pagan god, Dagon. The next morning, they found their pagan god Dagon fallen to his face. They put him back in place, and the next morning, they found him lying down with his head chopped off, both of his hands were gone and his legs were chopped to his knees.

"When the Philistines took the ark of God, they brought it into the house of Dagon, and set it by Dagon. And when they of Ashdod arose early on the morrow, behold, Dagon was fallen upon his face to the earth before the ark of the LORD. And they took Dagon, and set him in his place again. And when they arose early on the morrow morning, behold, Dagon was fallen upon his face to the ground before the ark of the LORD; and the head of Dagon and both the palms of his hands were cut off upon the threshold; only the stump of Dagon was left to him. The following morning the pagan god had fallen face down. The next morning the same thing happened, he had fallen down but his hand, feet and upper torso were broken" 1 Samuel 5:2-5.

Rayford J. Elliott

What was Jesus doing when the windstorm came down on the ship?

One day, Jesus got into a boat with His disciples and told them to go to the other side of the lake. As they began sailing, Jesus fell asleep. While he was sleeping, a storm came upon the waters. They woke Him up, and He rebuked the wind and the raging water and they ceased, and there was calm.

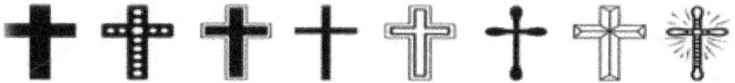

"Now it came to pass on a certain day, that he went into a ship with his disciples: and he said unto them, Let us go over unto the other side of the lake. And they launched forth. But as they sailed he fell asleep: and there came down a storm of wind on the lake; and they were filled with water, and were in jeopardy. And they came to him, and awoke him, saying, Master, master, we perish. Then he arose, and rebuked the wind and the raging of the water: and they ceased, and there was a calm" Luke 8:22-24.

How Well Do You Know the Holy Bible?

On what day of creation did God create man?

God created heaven and earth and all the universe. On the first day, He created light; on second day, He created the atmosphere and filament; on the third day, He created dry ground and planes; on the fourth day, He created the sun, moon, and stars; on the fifth day, He created birds and sea creatures, and on the sixth day, He created land animals and man. And of course, on the seventh day He rested, thus creating the Sabbath day.

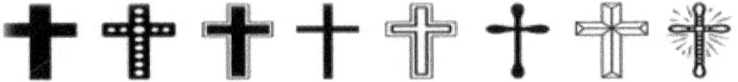

"Then God said, "Let Us make man in Our image, after Our likeness, to rule over the fish of the sea and the birds of the air, over the livestock, and over all the earth itself and every creature that crawls upon it." So God created man in His own image; in the image of God He created him; male and female He created them. God blessed them and said to them, "Be fruitful and multiply, and fill the earth and subdue it; rule over the fish of the sea and the birds of the air and every creature that crawls upon the earth" Genesis 1:26-28.

Rayford J. Elliott

How was sin forgiven in the Old Testament?

Sin is the act of being disobedient to the Word of God. It is what opened the pathway to hell, Satan's kingdom. On the other hand, Jesus is the Way for anyone to enter into heaven. He is the way. By the grace of God, He has given us the opportunity to be forgiven for sin and repent; this happens by the grace of God through faith. In the New Testament, sin is forgiven by God via Jesus Christ. All one needs to do is ask Him for forgiveness of his sin and repent. Jesus is faithful to forgive us. In the Old Testament, sin was handled differently. It was through atonement via animal sacrifices.

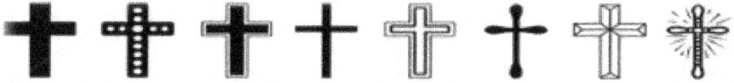

"And every day you shall offer a bull as a sin offering for atonement. Also you shall purify the altar, when you make atonement for it, and shall anoint it to consecrate it" Exodus 29:36.

"He shall also make restitution for what he has done amiss in the holy thing and shall add a fifth to it and give it to the priest. And the priest shall make atonement for him with the ram of the guilt offering, and he shall be forgiven" Leviticus 5:16.

Who did Jesus say His mother and brothers are?

After Jesus told His disciples the parable of the sower, but the disciples did not understand it. Jesus, therefore, explained it to them. Where they were meeting, He went on to tell them about the lamp under a jar and its meaning. Jesus' mother and brothers arrived. Someone told Jesus they were there. Jesus asked a rhetorical question; "Who is my mother and brother?" He explained that all who were present with him are his brothers. He explained all who hear his Word and do His Word are His brothers.

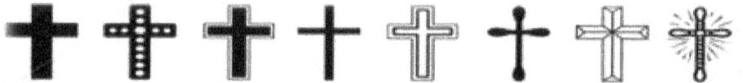

"Then came to him his mother and his brethren, and could not come at him for the press. And it was told him by certain which said, Thy mother and thy brethren stand without, desiring to see thee. And he answered and said unto them, My mother and my brethren are these which hear the word of God, and do it" Luke 18-21.

What did Hannah, Elkanah's wife, pray for at the doorstep of the temple while Eli was sitting in the chair watching?

Hannah was one of the two wives of Elkanah. Hannah was married for a long period of time but had not borne any children. However, by Elkanah's other wife, he had several children. Hanna went to the temple to pay. She prayed on the doorstep of the temple, and Eli was sitting next to the doorstep and saw her. He first thought was that she was drunk and asked her to get up. She kept praying, and Eli finally realized what she was doing. She was praying to the Lord to have mercy on her and give her a servant son. God answered her prayer.

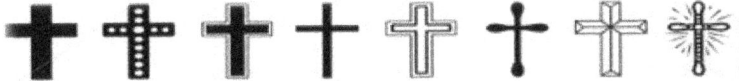

"After they had eaten and drunk in Shiloh, Hannah rose. Now Eli the priest was sitting on the seat beside the doorpost of the temple of the LORD*. "She was deeply distressed and prayed to the* LORD *and wept bitterly." And she vowed a vow and said, "O* LORD *of hosts, if you will indeed look on the affliction of your servant and remember me and not forget your servant, but will give to your servant a son, then I will give him to the* LORD *all the days of his life, and no razor shall touch his head"* 1 Samuel 1:9-11.

How many times did the people of Israel march around the city of Jericho?

One of the most important key things a believer in God can do is to have a discernment for the voice of God. God speaks to believers all the time, but one must be able to recognize His voice. God spoke to Joshua several times. Recognizing it was God, he carried out all of His commands. God told him and his people to march around the city Jericho one time each day for six days. And on the seventh day, they were to march around the city seven times that same day. That gave them a total of thirteen times they marched around the city of Jericho. That was the first city they captured in their quest for the Promise Land.

"Then the LORD said to Joshua, "See, I have delivered Jericho into your hands, along with its king and its fighting men. March around the city once with all the armed men. Do this for six days. Have seven priests carry trumpets of rams' horns in front of the ark. On the seventh day, march around the city seven times, with the priests blowing the trumpets" Joshua 6:2-4.

Rayford J. Elliott

Name three characters who used instruments in their battles to victory?

The scripture provides examples of many battles that were won in the Bible where the Word of God was carried out to achieve the victory. In practically each battle that was won, the sword, spear, chariot, and other common war equipment were used. There are three biblical characters who went to battle using other instrument to win their victory. Joshua used the trumpets, Gideon used trumpets and pitchers, and David used a sling shot as a major instrument that help win the battles against the Philistines.

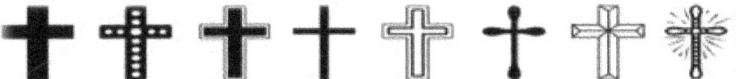

"And seven priests shall bear before the ark seven trumpets of rams' horns: and the seventh day ye shall compass the city seven times, and the priests shall blow with the trumpets" Joshua 6:4.
"So Gideon, and the hundred men that were with him, came unto the outside of the camp in the beginning of the middle watch; and they had but newly set the watch: and they blew the trumpets, and brake the pitchers that were in their hands" Judges 7:19.
"And David put his hand in his bag, and took thence a stone, and slang it, and smote the Philistine in his forehead, that the stone sunk into his forehead; and he fell upon his face to the earth." 1 Samuel 17:49.

What Paul did say that may "abound more and more in knowledge and in all judgment"?

One of the most admiral things about the apostle Paul is that he always supported what he established after his missionary journeys. One of the churches he established was the church in Philippi. He wrote letters and sent disciples to check on this established church of Jesus Christ. One letter he sent to show his solidarity and the love that he had for them. His love for Christ was the love he wanted them to have. If they abound in Christ and the gospel, they will abound in love. Through this, knowledge and judgment will abound in them.

"And this I pray, that your love may abound yet more and more in knowledge and in all judgment; That ye may approve things that are excellent; that ye may be sincere and without offence till the day of Christ. Being filled with the fruits of righteousness, which are by Jesus Christ, unto the glory and praise of God" Philippians 1:9-11.

Rayford J. Elliott

What did Solomon pay the wood cutters from Tyre who came to help build the temple?

In building the temple, King Solomon asked King Hiram of Tyre to send him skill craftsman and worker to help build the temple. Solomon was the richest man in the world. He paid them with 20,000 bushels of ground wheat, 20,000 bushels of barley, 20,000 bottles of wine, and 20,000 baths of olive oil.

"*And, behold, I will give to thy servants, the hewers that cut timber, twenty thousand measures of beaten wheat, and twenty thousand measures of barley, and twenty thousand baths of wine, and twenty thousand baths of oil*" 2 Chronicles 2:10.

How Well Do You Know the Holy Bible?

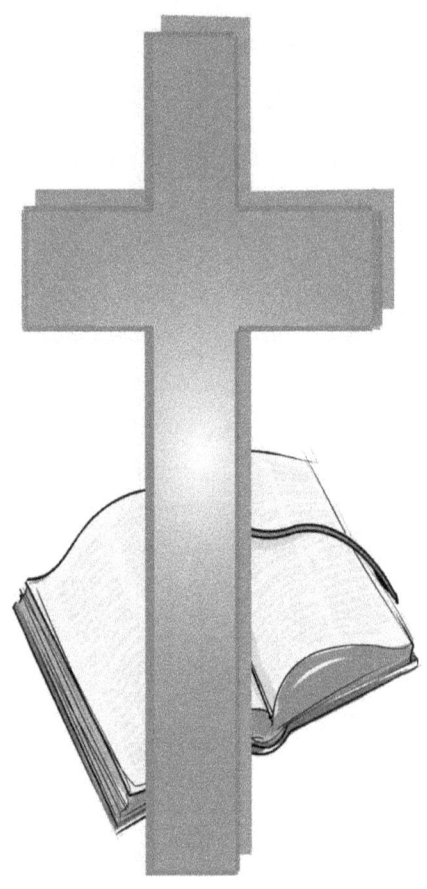

Rayford J. Elliott

Why did God cause the people who built the tower of Babel to speak different languages?

At one time the whole world spoke only one language. The people got together to build a tower called Babel, and they wanted it to "reach to heaven," so they would not have to scatter over the world. God saw what they were doing and did not approve. He wanted man to scatter the world and multiply. A common language is a characteristic that make up a nation. God came down and confused their language. As a result, they scattered, because they did understand each other in their communication.

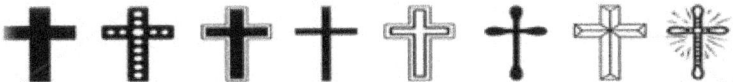

"Then they said, "Come, let us build ourselves a city, with a tower that reaches to the heavens, so that we may make a name for ourselves; otherwise we will be scattered over the face of the whole earth." But the LORD came down to see the city and the tower the people were building. The LORD said, "If as one people speaking the same language they have begun to do this, then nothing they plan to do will be impossible for them. Come, let us go down and confuse their language so they will not understand each other." So the LORD scattered them from there over all the earth, and they stopped building the city. that is why it was called Babel" Genesis 11:4-9.

How Well Do You Know the Holy Bible?

Who and what was included in the 10th plague that was brought upon Egypt?

After God had sent nine plagues down on Egypt, the Egyptians yet would not yield to the demand of God – "Let His people go." God Almighty proceeded to bring on one more plague, the tenth one. This one would surely have Pharaoh to yield to the demand shared by Moses. This final plague involved every first born in the land of Egypt who will die. This included the firstborn of Pharaoh the king, every slave girl and the firstborn of the cattle.

"Thus says the LORD: *'About midnight I will go out in the midst of Egypt, and every firstborn in the land of Egypt shall die, from the firstborn of Pharaoh who sits on his throne, even to the firstborn of the slave girl who is behind the handmill, and all the firstborn of the cattle"* Exodus 11:5.

Rayford J. Elliott

How many pieces of furniture were in the original tabernacle?

Moses was instructive by God at Mount Sinai to build the first tabernacle. This tabernacle was mobile. It was transported with the Israelites on their journey through the wilderness on their way to the Promise Land. After 440 years, Solomon's Temple superseded it as the dwelling place for God. There were four pieces in the tabernacle, three in the holy place.

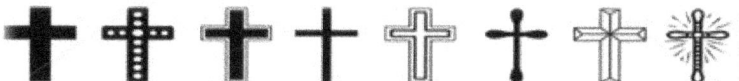

The following is a list of what was in the Temple.
- Altar of Burnt Offering (Exodus 27:1)
- Laver (Exodus 30:18)
- Table of Showbread (Exodus 25:23)
- Lampstand (Exodus 25:31)
- Altar of Incense (Exodus 30:1)
- Ark of the Covenant (Exodus 25:10)
- Mercy Seat (Exodus 25:17)

What did Lot offer the Sodomites outside of his house instead of the two angels who were spending the night in his home?

Lot had two men visitors who came to his home to warn him about what was about to happen to Sodom. When the Sodomites' men heard they were at Lot's house, they went to his home and demanded that Lot turn them over to them, so they could have sexual activity with them. Lot refused and told them instead that he had two virgin daughters and they could have them instead of the two men that was there.

"Lot went out to the men at the entrance, shut the door after him, and said, "I beg you, my brothers, do not act so wickedly. Behold, I have two daughters who have not known any man. Let me bring them out to you, and do to them as you please. Only do nothing to these men, for they have come under the shelter of my roof" Genesis 6:6-8.

Rayford J. Elliott

Where did Jesus kneel down and pray?

After Jesus foretold the denial of Peter and then taught that the scripture must be fulfilled in Him, he went up to the Mount of Olives. The disciples followed him there. After they arrived, He told them to pray that they would not be led into temptation. He departed from them. Approximately forty or fifty yards away from their camp, He knelt down and prayed.

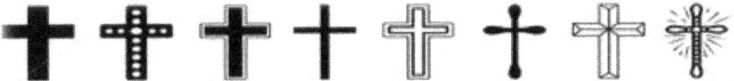

"And he came out, and went, as he was wont, to the mount of Olives; and his disciples also followed him. And when he was at the place, he said unto them, Pray that ye enter not into temptation. And he was withdrawn from them about a stone's cast, and kneeled down, and prayed" Luke 22:39-41.

Which prophet was assigned by God to be the watchman?

Ezekiel was a prophet and a special messenger for God. He was called to take special messages to His people. He prepared him to deliver His messages. In preparation, God first filled him with the Word. The Bible described this process as Ezekiel eating his scroll (The Word). He took the message of God to the people in captivity at Telabib near a river. He was there for seven days. Afterward, God told him that He would make him a watchman for His people.

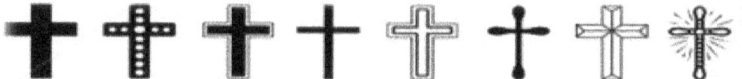

"Son of man," He added, *"listen carefully to all the words I speak to you, and take them to heart. Go to your people, the exiles; speak to them and tell them, 'This is what the Lord GOD says,' whether they listen or refuse to listen"* Ezekiel 3:10-11.

"And it came to pass at the end of seven days, that the word of the LORD came unto me, saying, Son of man, I have made thee a watchman unto the house of Israel" Ezekiel 3:16-17.

Which two prophets wept over the city of Jerusalem?

When Jesus was making His triumphal entry into Jerusalem, He rode the colt that two of His disciples had fetched for Him. Some disciples spread out their cloak along the way and praised God joyfully with a loud voice. The Pharisees heard and asked Jesus to make them stop. Jesus then felt for the city of Jerusalem and wept for the city. The other prophet is Jeremiah. Known as the weeping prophet, he wept for Jerusalem because of its apostasy state.

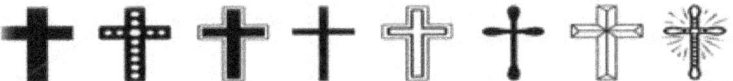

"And some of the Pharisees from among the multitude said unto him, Master, rebuke thy disciples. And he answered and said unto them, I tell you that, if these should hold their peace, the stones would immediately cry out. And when he was come near, he beheld the city, and wept over it" Luke 23:39-40.

"Mine heart within me is broken because of the prophets; all my bones shake; I am like a drunken man, and like a man whom wine hath overcome, because of the LORD, and because of the words of his holiness. For the land is full of adulterers; for because of swearing the land mourneth; the pleasant places of the wilderness are dried up, and their course is evil, and their force is not right" Jeremiah 23:9-10.

Which two books in the Bible end with a question?

There are 66 books in the Bible. In the King James Version, there are 39 books in the Old Testament and 27 Books in the New Testament. Each book written was spiritually inspired. There are two unique ones that end with a question. They are Jonah and Nahum. However, both books have to do with the city of Nineveh. Nahum ends with a question about God's punishment of Nineveh, and Jonah ends with a question about God's pity for Nineveh.

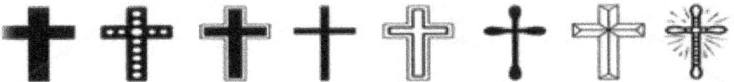

"And should not I spare Nineveh, that great city, wherein are more than six score thousand persons that cannot discern between their right hand and their left hand; and also much cattle?" Jonah 4:11.
"There is no healing of thy bruise; thy wound is grievous: all that hear the bruit of thee shall clap the hands over thee: for upon whom hath not thy wickedness passed continually?" Nahum 3:19.

Who was the first to preach to the gentiles?

God chose and trusted the Jewish people with His Word and to spread it throughout all the lands. However, many times, they misconstrued the responsibility. They were knowledgeable of God's Word but refused to spread it to others outside the Jewish nation. But there was one prophet who unwillingly took the Word to the Gentiles (Gentile is a name that is given to people that are not of the Jewish race). That was the prophet Jonah. He preached repentance to the city of Nineveh, an Assyrian city. The people of that city listened to Jonah's message from God and repented. By doing so, it kept the city from being destroyed by God because of their sinful living.

"And the word of the LORD came unto Jonah the second time, saying, Arise, go unto Nineveh, that great city, and preach unto it the preaching that I bid thee. So Jonah arose, and went unto Nineveh, according to the word of the LORD. Now Nineveh was an exceeding great city of three days' journey. And Jonah began to enter into the city a day's journey, and he cried, and said, Yet forty days, and Nineveh shall be overthrown" Jonah 3: 1-4.

How many gathered in the upper room and how many were apostles?

After the ascension of Jesus, the disciples left Mount Olive and returned to Jerusalem, which requires a day of traveling. When they arrived, they all met in a place called the Upper Room. There was a total of 120 disciples, eleven were apostles, including the women, Mary, the mother of Jesus, and with His brothers.

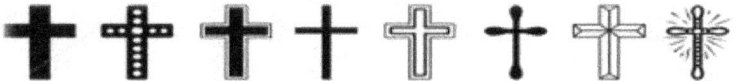

"Then they returned to Jerusalem from the Mount of Olives, which is near the city, a Sabbath day's journey away. When they arrived, they went to the upper room where they were staying: Peter and John, James and Andrew, Philip and Thomas, Bartholomew and Matthew, James son of Alphaeus, Simon the Zealot, and Judas son of James. With one accord they all continued in prayer, along with the women and Mary the mother of Jesus, and with His brothers. In those days Peter stood up among the brothers (a gathering of about a hundred and twenty) and said" Acts 1:12-15.

How Well Do You Know the Holy Bible?

Rayford J. Elliott

How does Jesus make us righteous?

In the Old Testament, the patriarchs were counted righteousness by God. Abraham for example, with his strong faith and obedience to God, was counted righteous by God. In the advent of our Lord and Savor Jesus Christ who died to bare our sin, we are made righteous through Him who knew no sin.

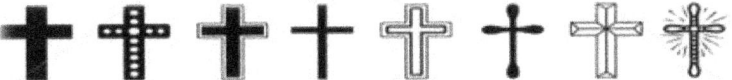

"*Now then we are ambassadors for Christ, as though God did beseech you by us: we pray you in Christ's stead, be ye reconciled to God. For he hath made him to be sin for us, who knew no sin; that we might be made the righteousness of God in*" 2 Corinthians 5:21-22.

Deliverance Prayer

Lord, how many are my foes!
How many rise up against me!
Many are saying of me,
"God will not deliver him."
But you, Lord, are a shield around me,
my glory, the One who lifts my head high.
I call out to the Lord,
and he answers me from his holy mountain.
I lie down and sleep;
I wake again, because the Lord sustains me.
I will not fear though tens of thousands
assail me on every side.
Arise, Lord!
Deliver me, my God!
Strike all my enemies on the jaw;
break the teeth of the wicked.
From the Lord comes deliverance.
May your blessing be on your people.

List of Commonly Committed Sins and Their Causes
*Bible verses used from ESV, NIV, KJV, and Topical Bible.

abandonment	Psalm 34:18
abduction	Deuteronomy 24:7
abhorring judgment	Leviticus 26:43-44
abomination	Leviticus 20:13
abortion	Exodus 20:21-25
abusiveness	2 Peter 1:4
abhorrence of holy things	Act 2:33
accusation	Jude 1:9
adulterous lust	Matthew 5:27-28
adultery	Proverb 6:24-29
afflicting others	Isaiah 58:1-14
aggravation	Genesis 2:24
agitation	Proverb 12:25
aiding and abetting sin	**Colossians 3:12-17**
alcoholism	Galatians 5:21
all unrighteousness	1 John 1:9
anger	James 1:20
animosity	Ephesians 4:32
anxiety	Peter 5:6-7
apprehension	Thessalonians 1:1-12
argumentativeness	Timothy 2:15
arrogance	1Samuel 2:3
assaults	2 Samuel 13:1-39
astrology	Deuteronomy 28:9-12
atheism	Psalm 14:1
avariciousness	1 Timothy 6:9

Baal worship	2 Kings 17:16
backbiting	Proverbs 16:28
backsliding	Corinthians 13:5
bad attitude	Psalm 104:19
bad language	Ephesians 4:29
bearing false witness	Proverbs 19:5
big talk	Hebrews 10:25
being a workaholic	Proverbs 23:4
being quick to speak	Proverbs 17:28
belittling	Isaiah 55:8-9;
bereavement	Thessalonians 4:13
betraying Jesus	Matthew 27:3
bickering	Philippians 2:14
bigotry	Galatians 3:28 1
bitterness	Ephesians 4:31-32
black magic	Deuteronomy 18:9-14
blackmail	1 Corinthians 6:9-11
blasphemy	Matthew 12:31-32
boastfulness	Matthew 6:1-2
boisterousness	Exodus 23:1
bow to images	1 Timothy 2:5
bragging	Matthew 6:1-34
brainwashing	Philippians 4:8
break His commands	John 14:23-24
break his covenants	Luke 22:30
breaking covenants w/others	Hebrews 13:4
bribery	Exodus 23:8
brutality	Matthew 10:17-18
burn incense to gods	Leviticus 10:1-2
calamity	Isaiah 45:7 Job 2:10
carelessness	Timothy 2:15
cars/riches of world	Matthew 6:24

carnality	1 Corinthians 3:3
casting God away	1 John 4:1
cause disagreements	Colossians 2:1-23
causing distress	2 Thessalonians 2:1-7
causing division	Romans 16:17-18
causing fear	John 14:27
causing men to err	John 10:1-42
causing offense	Corinthians 8:1-13
causing poor to fail	Luke 14:12-14
changing truth to lies	John 8:44
chanting of charms	Deuteronomy 18:9-12
cheating	James 4:17
come against His anointed	1 Samuel 24:6
complaining	Philippians 2:14
complacency	Proverb 1:23
conceit	Romans 12:16
concupiscence	Colossians 3:5
condemnation	Roman 8:1
condemning the just	Ephesians 4:32
causing conflict	Ephesians 4:32
confrontation	Matthew 18:15-20
confusion	Timothy 2:7
conjuration	Timothy 4:1
conspiring against God	Roman 13:1-14
consulting wizards	Leviticus 19:31
contempt	Romans 14:1-23
contention	Proverbs 3:30
controlling	2 Peter 1:5-8
conniving	Proverb 6:16-19
compulsiveness	Corinthians 9:27
contentiousness	Corinthians 11:16
contesting and resisting God	1 Timothy 3:1-7

corruption	2 Peter 2:19
counterfeiting Chris. work	2 Corin. 11:13-15
covering sin	Roman 6:33
coveting	Exodus 20:17
covetousness	Timothy 6:6-11
cravenness	Proverbs 23:31
criticalness	Colossians 3:12-14
crookedness	Proverb 11:3
cruelty	Proverb 12:10
using crystals	Acts 8:9-13
cursing God	Matthew 10:32-33
cursing	Ephesians 4:29
dealing treacherously	Romans 7:3
deceit	Proverbs 20:17
deception	Galatians 6:7-8
defamation	Titus 3:1-2
defeatism	Ephesians 6:10-18
defiantness	Genesis 3:1-24
defiling	Leviticus 15:31
degrading	Romans 1:24
dejection	Proverb 29:23
demon consciousness	Acts 16:16-18
demon worship	Ephesians 6:10-13
deny Jesus, resurrection	Matthew 10:33
dependencies	1 Thessalonians 4:12
depravity	Romans 1:29
desecration	Ezekiel 7:22
desires of this world	Colossians 3:5
despair	Isaiah 19:9
despising God	Samuel 2:30
despitefulness	Leviticus 20:13
despondency	Galatians 6:9

deviousness	Proverb 2:16
disagreements	Ephes. 4:31-5:2
disbelief	Mark 9:24
discord	Proverb 6:16-19
discrediting	2 Peter 1:21
discouragement	Exodus 6:9
disdain	Proverb 23:22
disgust	Ezekiel 23:17
dishonesty	Colossians 3:9-10
disobedience	Deuteronomy 28:15
disorderly	2 Thessalonians 3:6
disputing	1 Timothy 2:8
disrespectfulness	Corinthians 15:33
disruptive	1 John 2:15
dissension	Proverb 6:14
distantness	Deuteronomy 30:4
distrust	2 Timothy 3:16
division	1 Corinthians 1:10-13
divorce	Deuteronomy 24:1
domineering	Galatians 3:28
double-talking	1 Peter 5:8
double mindedness	James 1:6-8
doubt	Proverbs 3:5-8
dread	Deuteronomy 7:21
drug abuse	1 Corinthians 6:19
drunkenness	Proverbs 20:1
duplicity	Proverbs 6:16-19
drinking blood	Genesis 9:30
eating blood	Deuteronomy 12:33
eating unclean food	Acts 10:14
effeminate behavior	Deuteronomy 6:9
egotism	Philippians 2:1-10

enlarged imaginations	2 Corinthians 10:5
enter unrighteous agreements	Hosea 10:4
envy	Job 5:2
escaping	1 Corinthians 10:13
evil hearts & imaginations	2 Thessalonians 3:2
exasperation	Ephesians 4:1-3
extortion	Leviticus 6:4
failure in duty	Genesis 38:8
failure to glorify God	Psalm 69:12, 86:12
falsehood	Job 21:34
fantasizing	James 1:14-15
fault finding	John 7:24
fear	2 Timothy 1:7
fear of disapproval	2 Kings 8:19
fear of man	Proverb 29:25
fetishes	Romans 7:8
fighting	Proverb 28:25
flattery	Proverbs 29:5
foolishness	Corinthians 1:18
folly	Job 42:8; Psalm 69:5
forcefulness	Matthew 11:12
fornication	1 Corinthians 7:2
fortune telling	Leviticus 19:3
fraud	Luke 16:10-13
fretting	1 Peter 5:5-7
frustrations	2 Samuel 13:2
fury	Job 40:11
giving offense	Genesis 20:16
gloominess	Zephaniah 1:15
gluttony	Proverbs 23:2
gossip	Proverbs 11:13, 20:19
greed	Matthew 23:25

grieving	Nehemiah 8:10, 8:11
grumbling	Exodus 16:7
guilt	Hosea 13:16
harlotry	Nahum 3:4
harshness	Malachi 3:13
hating God	Exodus 20:5
hating	Titus 3:3; Jude 1:23
haughtiness	Jeremiah 48:29
high-minded	1 Corinthians 1:19
homosexuality	1 Corinthians 6:9
hopeless	Isaiah 57:10
horoscopes	Leviticus 19:31
human sacrifice	Deuteronomy 18:20
hypocrisy	Matthew 23:28
idleness	2 Thessalonians 3:6
idle words, deeds, & actions	Matthew 12:36-37
idolatries	Jeremiah 14:14
ill will	Deuteronomy 15:9
inhumanity	1 John 3:15
imaginations	2 Corinthians 10:5
immorality	Jeremiah 3:9; Jude 1:4
impatience	James 5:7-8
impetuousness	Habakkuk 1:6
imprudence	Proverbs 14:8, 14:15
impurity	Leviticus 15:19
inadequacy	2 Corinthians 12:9
incest	Leviticus 18:6-18
incitement	Proverbs 29:11
indifferences	Revelation 3:15-16
inflating	Matthew 7:1
inflexibility	Philippians 4:1-23
inhospitality	Ezekiel 16:49-50

iniquity in your heart	Psalm 25:11; 51:9
injustice	Micah 6:8
insolence	Titus 3:2
intemperance	Proverbs 23:29-35
intentional sins	Hebrews 10:26
intimidation	Nehemiah 6:13-14
intolerances	2 Samuel 12:7
intellectualism, sophisticated	1 Timothy 6:20
inventing sin	James 1:4; Acts 2:28
inventing evil	Romans 1:24-32
inward wickedness	Ephesians 6:12
irrationality	Roman 1:20
irreverence	Nehemiah 5:15
jealousy	Exodus 34:14
being judgmental	Luke 6:37
justifying the wicked	Proverbs 11:1
kidnapping	Deuteronomy 24:7
killing	1 Samuel 19:5
lack of self-control	1 Corinthians 7:9
lawlessness	1 John 3:4; James 4:17
lasciviousness	Proverbs 2:16-18
laziness	Proverbs 12:24
lesbianism	Romans 1:27-27
levitation	Isaiah 60:1, 60:8
lewdness	Ephesians 5:5
lying	Proverbs 12:22
loathing	Psalm 119:158
longing for sin	1 Peter 2:1-25
loneliness	Psalm 25:16
loose morals	James 1:12
looting	1 Samuel 23:1
loving evil	Psalm 52:3

loving money	Matthew 6:24
loving praise	Philippians 2:3-4
lust	Matthew 5:28
lust of the eye	Matthew 5:28
lust of the flesh	1 John 2:16
lust of the mind	Psalm 25:11
lying to the Holy Spirit	Acts 5:1-5
lying with pleasure & delight	Colossians 3:9-10
madness	John 10:20
magic	Acts 8:9-13
making war	Micah 3:5
maliciousness	Exodus 23:1
manipulation	Galatians 2:4
manslaughter	Matthew 5:21
marauding	Joshua 8:27
masturbation	James 1:14-15
materialism	Luke 12:15
mischief	Ephesians 4:1-3
misery	Exodus 3:7
misleading	Matthew 18:6-7
mulishness	Leviticus 26:19
mocking	Proverbs 17:5
murder	Exodus 20:13
murmuring	Philippians 2:14
muttering	Isaiah 8:19
necromancy	Leviticus 19:31
negativism	Matthew 7:1-2
nicotine addiction	1 Corinthians 6:19
not being watchful	Matthew 24:24
occultism	Isaiah 8:18
obsessing	2 Corinthians 10:4-5
obstinacy	1 John 3:2

oppression	Deuteronomy 26:7
overbearing	Titus 1:7
pedophilia	Leviticus 18:23
persecuting believers	2 Timothy 3:12
persecuting, persecution	Acts 9:11
perversion	Leviticus 18:23
perverting the gospel	Acts 20:20
petulance	Isaiah 40:32
planning without God	Proverbs 16:9
plotting	Ezekiel 11:2
plundering	Ezekiel 39:10
pompousness	1 Timothy 4:13
pornography	Psalm 101:3
possessiveness	Mark 12:27
pouting	Proverbs 14:17; 15:18
prayerlessness	1 Thessalonians 5:17
prejudice	Galatians 3:28
presumption	2 Peter 3:1-18
pretend to be a prophet	2 Peter 2:1-22
pretension	2 Corinthians 10:5
pridefulness	Proverbs 11:2
pride of life	1 John 2:16
procrastination	1 Peter 5:7
profane God	Colossians 3:8
profanity unto God	1 Timothy 6:10
professing to be wise	James 1:1-27
prophecy by Baal	Deuteronomy 18:15
prophesying lies	1 John 4:1
propagating lies	Exodus 5:9
proudness	James 4:6
provoking God	Deuteronomy 4:25
provoking	Galatians 5:26

puffing up	1 Samuel 17:28
quarreling	Genesis 13:8
quenching the Holy Spirit	Solomon 8:7
questioning God's Word	Isaiah 55:8-9
raiding	Proverbs 24:15
railing	Proverb 102.8
raging	Psalm 37:8
raping	Deut. 22:25-28
rationalization	Luke 14:18-20
ravaging	1 Chronicles 21:12
rebellion	Psalm 106:43
rebuking	2 Timothy 3:16
recklessness	Numbers 22:32
refusing to hear	Matthew 11:15
refusing to repent	Jeremiah 15:19
refusing to be humble	1 Chronicles 7:14
refusing to live in peace	Roman 5:1
rejecting reproof, salvation	Proverbs 5:12, 6:23
rejecting God and His Word	Luke 9:23
rejection	Romans 11:15
rejoicing in others' adversity	Colossians 2:18
rejoicing in idols	1 Corinthians 10:14
rejoicing in iniquity	John 14:1-31
repetitiveness	Hebrews 10:26
reproaching good men	Job 27:6
resentment	Judges 8:3
restlessness	Genesis 4:12
retaliation	Matthew 5:39
reveling	1 Samuel 30:16
reviling	Matthew 5:11, 15:4
revenge	Leviticus 19:18
rigidity	Mark 9:18

robbing God	Malachi 3:8
robbery	Philippians 2:6
rudeness	Matthew 5:22
sadism	Nahum 3:19
scheming	Ester 9:25
scornfulness	1 Samuel 2:29
seduction	Acts 18:13
seeking self-gain	Matthew 6:33
seek pleasures from world	Matthew 6:33
self-accusations	1 Corinthians 3:16-17
self-admiration	1 Corinthians 3:16-17
self-centeredness	Matthew 16:24
self-condemnation	1 Peter 3:3-4
self-corruption	Luke 16:15
self-criticalness	Proverbs 12:18
self-deception	2 Peter 3:9
self-delusion	Titus 1:11-12
self-destruction	Matthew 7:13-14
self-exultation	Isaiah 45:25
self-glorification	Psalm 34:3
self-hatred	Ephesians 5:29
self-importance	Galatians 2:6
self-rejection	Psalm 34:17-20
selfishness	Philippians 2:4
self-pity	1 Thessalonians 5:18
self-righteousness	Luke 18:9-14
self-seeking	Romans 2:8
serving other gods	Joshua 24:15
sewing discord	Proverbs 6:16-19
sexual idolatry	Matthew 5:28
sexual immorality	Thessalonians 4:2-8
sexual impurity	Thessalonians 4:3-5

sexual perversion	Leviticus 18:23
oral sex	1 Corinthians 7:3-4
sodomy	Leviticus 20:13
shame	Isaiah 61:7
silliness	Proverbs 8:5
sinful mirth	Job 20:5
skepticism	Matthew 21:21
slander	Leviticus 19:16
slaying	Psalm 34:21
slothfulness	Proverbs 6:6, 19:15
snobbishness	Romans 12:16
soothsaying	Leviticus 20:6
sorcery	Leviticus 19:31
sowing seeds of hatred	James 4:11; 6:14
speaking curses	Isaiah 8:10
speaking incantations	Ezekiel 13:20
speaking folly	Job 42:8; Psalm 38:5
speculation	Matthew 12:37
spell-casting	Matthew 10:28
spiritual laziness	Proverbs 19:16
spitefulness	1 Peter 2:1-25
stealing	Ephesians 4:28
stiff-necked	Exodus 32:9
strife	Proverbs 20:3
striving over leadership	Colossians 3:23-24
struggling	1 Corinthians 10:13
stubbornness	Psalm 81:11-12
stupidity	Romans 1:22
suicidal thoughts	James 4:7
suspicion	Hebrews 11:6
swearing	James 5:12
take advantage of others	Luke 6:31

taking a bribe	Exodus 23:8
taking offense	Samuel 25:28
take God's Name in vain	Matthew 12:23
taking rights from poor	Ezekiel 18:16,18
teaching false doctrines	1 Timothy 1:3, 6:3
temper	1 Samuel 20:7
temptation	Matthew 6:13, 26:14
tempting God	James 1:13
theft	Matthew 15:19
timidity	2 Timothy 1:7
trickery, two-facedness	Genesis 3:1
trustless	Numbers 20:12
trusting lies	Psalm 118:8
trust own righteousness	John 14:1
trusting wickedness	John 12:36
tumults	Amos 2:2
turn your back on God	Matthew 10:33
unbelief	Mark 9:24
unbridled lust	Thessalonians 4:4
uncleanness	Matthew 12:43
uncompromising	James 4:17
undermining	Job 15:4
unequal yoked no-believers	2 Corinthians 6:14
unfairness	Matthew 20:13
unfaithfulness	Leviticus 6:2
un-forgiveness	Mark 11:25
unfriendliness	Proverbs 18:1
ungratefulness	Luke 6:35
unholy alliances	1 Kings 3:1
unholy habits	Timothy 5:13
unmanly	Genesis 1:26
unmercifulness	Matthew 18:21

unrepentant	1 John 1:9; Rev. 2:5
unrighteousness	Jeremiah 22:13
unruliness of tongues	Micah 6:13
usury	Nehemiah 5:10, 5:7
unthankful	Colossians 3:15, 4:2
untruthfulness	Proverbs 12:17, 14:5
Unworthiness	Luke 17:10
using tarot cards	Leviticus 20:6
vain imaginations	Zachariah 10:2
vanity	1 Samuel 16:7
vengeance	Romans 12:19
viciousness	Matthew 26:52-54
violence	Job 16:17; Oba. 1:10
vulgarity	Ephesians 4:29, 5:4
white magic	Leviticus 19:31
wickedness	Timothy 5:8
willful sin	Hebrews 10:26
willful, intentional sin	Numbers 3:1-51
winking with evil intent	Job 15:12; Prov. 3:29
witchcraft, withdrawal	Deuter. 18:9-12, 18:20
withholding a pledge	Proverb 3:27, 23:13
without concern	Timothy 6:20
without natural affection	John 13:34-35
without mercy	Luke 6:36
working for praise	Galatians 5:16-26
worldliness	1 John 2:15-17
worrying	Matthew 6:25-34
worshipping possessions	Revelation 9:20
worshipping our works	Roman 1:25
worshipping the creation	Roman 1:25
worshipping of planets	John 4:23
wrathfulness	Psalm 37:8

wrong doing Exodus 23:2
zealous make others sinful Romans 10:2
zealousness in outward show Philippians 1:27

References

Bible Gateway. biblegateway.com. January 2019

Zondervan. (2003). NIV Quest Study Bible, Revised, Rapid, Michigan 49530.

The Holy Bible. (1998). KJV Holman Bible Publishers, Nashville, Tennessee.

Amplified Translation. biblegateway.org

King James Translation. biblegateway.org

New King James Version.

New Living Translation. biblehub.com

KJV Holman Study Bible. (2012). Holman Bible publisher. Nashville, Tennessee.

Psalm 3, David deliverance prayer.

About the Author

Elder Rayford Jones Elliott is a minister of the gospel of Jesus Christ. He is a devout follower of Christ Jesus because he loves the Lord with his whole heart. As a minister, he teaches and preaches the Word with great fervency in an attempt to save the lost by bringing them into the knowledge of the truth. In his local church, where he has been a member for eighteen years, Elder Elliott serves as the president of the Men's Fellowship and men's Sunday school teacher. He conducts weekly discussion groups, thereby demonstrating his dedication to the spiritual development of men. It is his desire to instill in them the same love and zeal for Christ Jesus that he possesses.

www.ingramcontent.com/pod-product-compliance
Lightning Source LLC
Chambersburg PA
CBHW032131090426
42743CB00007B/555